Certain Young Men

Peter Gill was born in 1939 in Cardiff and started his professional career as an actor. A director as well as a writer, he has directed over eighty productions in the UK, Europe and North America. At the Royal Court Theatre in the sixties, he was responsible for introducing D. H. Lawrence's plays to the theatre. Of *Small Change*, *The Times* said: 'This is a beautiful product of uncompromising puritan imagination.' Peter Gill lives in London and was an Associate Director of the Royal National Theatre, 1980–97. The founding director of Riverside Studios and the Royal National Theatre Studio, his last play, *Cardiff East*, was produced at the Cottesloe Theatre in 1997. His new play for young people, *Friendly Fire*, will be produced in 1999.

PETER GILL

Certain Young Men

faber and faber

First published in 1999
by Faber and Faber Limited
3 Queen Square, London WC1N 3AU

Typeset by Country Setting, Kingsdown, Kent CT14 8ES
Printed in England by Intype London Ltd

A CIP record for this book
is available from the British Library

ISBN 0–571–20191–1

2 4 6 8 10 9 7 5 3 1

Characters

Stewart

Michael

David

Christopher

Andrew

Tony

Robert

Terry

*Suggestion of a room able to include
all the locations indicated.*

*On the floor: books, records, clothes, magazines,
newspapers, video tapes, cups, beer cans, etc.*

No furniture except perhaps for chairs when necessary.

*After the characters make their first entrance,
they remain on stage during the rest of the play.*

In memory of Michael

Certain Young Men was first performed at the Almeida Theatre, London, on 21 January 1999 with the following cast:

Stewart Alec Newman
Michael John Light
David Jeremy Northam
Christopher Andrew Woodall
Andrew Andrew Lancel
Tony Peter Sullivan,
Robert Sean Chapman
Terry Danny Dyer

Direction Peter Gill
Design Nathalie Gibbs
Light Hartley T. A. Kemp
Sound Frank Bradlev
Casting Toby Whale
Costume Supervisor Charlotte Stuart

And there followed him a certain young man,
having a linen cloth cast about his naked body;
and the young man laid hold of him:

And he left the linen cloth and fled from them naked.

St Mark, XIV, 51–52

ONE

Stewart and Michael.

Stewart Right then.

Michael Are you going to ring?

Stewart I said I'd ring.

Michael But are you going to?

Stewart Yeah. Of course I am, what's the matter with you?

Michael I'd better give you the right number then.

Stewart I've got it.

Michael No you haven't. Here.

He takes a piece of paper with the number on it from Stewart.

Stewart Well fuck me.

Michael Yeah.

Stewart What you do that for? What a liberty. What you do that for? Fuck me.

Michael Haven't you ever done that?

Stewart No I haven't got a phone. Anyway I wouldn't. Why did you do that?

Michael I don't know. In case you rang. I don't know.

Stewart But you asked me to ring.

Michael I know. Will you ring?

Stewart I dunno now.

Michael I thought you wouldn't.

Stewart I said I fucking would. Where's the number?

Michael Where's my pen. I can't find my pen. You got a pen?

Stewart gives him a pen.

Thanks.

He writes the number down and gives Stewart back the paper and pen. Stewart takes the paper and pen; the top comes off. Michael is left holding the pen.

Stewart Honest. You. Honest.

He retrieves the pen and puts the top back on.

Michael There we are. Thanks.

Stewart Right then.

Michael You off?

Stewart Yes.

Michael Are you going to ring?

Stewart I said I would.

Michael Or . . .

Stewart Do you want to leave it then?

Michael If you want to.

Stewart Do you want to? Give me your number.

Michael Or perhaps . . .

Stewart Well I'm off . . . I'll phone you . . . Shall I?

Michael Sorry? What? Oh, yes. You've got the number have you?

Stewart Yes. Oh no. Where is it? What did I do with it?

Michael picks up a scrap of paper from the floor and gives it to him.

Oh yeah. Thanks. I'll see you then.

Michael Yes.

Stewart Thank you for the . . .

Michael Oh that's . . . Listen, ring first OK? Don't . . .

Stewart No.

Michael It might be . . .

Stewart Yeah.

Michael You probably won't ring anyway.

Stewart What do you say that for? You never know. Do you? Eh? Anyway thanks. OK?

Michael Yes.

Stewart And I'm sorry about the . . .

Michael Oh that's . . . Listen take care.

Stewart Of what?

Michael I wonder if he'll ring. He might ring. He won't ring. Why should he ring? What if he rings?

Stewart Have you given me the wrong number?

Michael No.

Stewart Only I noticed the number when I came in. You gonna muck me about?

Michael Or . . .
Do you want the number?

Stewart No.

Michael Or . . .
Do you want the number?

Stewart No. Thanks.

Michael Or . . .

Stewart Here we are. OK?

Michael What's your name?

Stewart Stewart.

Michael You don't look like a Stewart.
Do you charge?

Stewart What?

Michael You should charge. You've got the kind of flat
and the kind of records. And you live in the kind of
street.

Stewart What?

Michael It's so beautiful this street.

Stewart What are you called?

Michael Stewart.

Stewart No. Come on. Come on.

He moves towards Michael.

Michael No.

Michael looks front, as if out of a window.

It's so beautiful this street in this weather.

Stewart Is it? If you think so.

He moves away.

Michael I do. What are they, the trees?

Stewart Trees. Street trees. Are you a student?

Michael I wonder they haven't sold these off. These flats. These cold water flats.

Stewart Why?

Michael They generally do. Sell them.

Stewart Oh yeah.

Michael They do. Do them up. Sell them. They do.

Stewart What do you mean cold water flats? This isn't a cold water flat.

Michael That's what they are.

Stewart You're not in New York you know. What *do* you do then?

Michael I like these flats up all those stone stairs. Do you have neighbours?

Stewart Why won't you tell me?

Michael I like the door knob, the broken glass.

Stewart Eh?

Michael This is just the kind of flat where the guy's on the game.

Stewart Do you want to pay?

Michael Yeah.
 Or . . .

Stewart I might see you then.

Michael Or . . .

Stewart Thanks.

Michael Or . . .

Stewart No. I'm not.

Michael Or . . .

Stewart Look at all these books.

Michael Or . . .

Stewart I'm off then.

Michael Or . . .

Stewart Do you want to leave it then?

Michael Or . . .

Stewart D'you wanna leave it then?

Michael Or . . .

Stewart Do you wanna leave it then?

Michael I don't know, do you?

Stewart I don't mind, do you?

Michael I don't know, do you?

Stewart I don't mind, do you?

Michael I don't know.
  Or . . .

Stewart Shall I see you then?

Michael Perhaps.

Stewart See you then.

Michael Or . . .

Stewart I can see when you're excited.

Michael Or . . .

Stewart I've got plans for you.

Michael Or . . .

Stewart What are you in to?

Michael I'm in to you at the moment. What are you in to?

Stewart Yeah.

Michael Or . . .

Stewart No I'm not.

Michael Or . . .

Stewart Are you scared? What are you scared of?

Michael Or it could be . . .

Stewart Ssh . . . Ssh.

Stewart leads Michael by the arm.

Michael What?

Stewart You'll wake him up.

Michael Who?

Stewart Lenny.

Michael Christ! Who's he?

Stewart The fella I share with.

Michael What?

Stewart Ssh, come on. He won't wake up. He won't mind if he does. He'll be quite happy.

Michael No.

Stewart Yeah! Come on.

Stewart begins to unbuckle his belt.

Michael Or . . .

Stewart Right then!

Michael Oh yes!

Stewart I'm off then.

He doesn't go.

OK?

No response.

OK?

Michael What? Oh yes. Yes.
Or . . .

Stewart Do you want me to ring?

Michael Or . . .
Why don't you ring?

Stewart No. I won't bother.

Michael Or . . .

Stewart Are we here then?

Michael Or . . .

Stewart This is it, then?

Michael Or . . .

Stewart Do you live by yourself?

Michael Or . . .

Stewart Is this all yours then?

Michael Or . . .

Stewart I don't want to hurt you.

Michael Or . . .

Stewart Are you a student?

TWO

Christopher is sitting, smoking a cigarette and reading. David is standing.

David What is it?
  Chris.

Christopher What?

David What's the matter?

Christopher What do you mean what's the matter. I'm reading.

David Oh dear.

Christopher I'm alright, honest. What is it?
  David.

David It's alright. It's alright.

Christopher Oh Christ. Come on. What?

David Nothing. Give us.

  David takes Christopher's cigarette. Christopher lights another.

Christopher I thought you weren't supposed to smoke. You're always telling me not to smoke.

David Well you shouldn't smoke.
  I thought you'd look nice in a punt.

Christopher I come from Oxford. I didn't go to Oxford.

You went to Oxford.
 It was a nice afternoon. It was.

David No it wasn't.

Christopher Well it doesn't matter does it?

David Thanks.

Christopher Oh Christ.

David Can I have a drink?

Christopher Yeah.

David What have we got?

Christopher What have we got? You can have lager or extra strong lager.

David Yeah.

   Christopher goes out.

You think this is it. You think this is . . . Smudge of oil on his cheek. That's the way his hair falls when parted. This is . . . him.
 I see him go from startled laughing unbelieving boy to junker-headed sensualist.

   Christopher comes in with two cans of lager.

How's that other car?

Christopher OK. OK.

David Nearly finished?

Christopher Very nearly.

David Alvis. Another Alvis?

Christopher Yes another. Greylady.

David Why do you work in a garage?

Christopher What's this now? Why do you work in a hospital? I like working in a garage. What do you want me to do, take a course as a wheelwright?

David That's not what you said yesterday. Don't you want money?

Christopher No I don't want money. Do you? You don't have any money.

David No. But I'm not short of money. You must have earned money.

Christopher I did alright. It's in the house. She's got the house OK? It's hers. Do you want more money. From me?

David No.

Christopher Well shut up then.

I used to work with people who would have gone to a party on the Marchioness. Girls in advertising who eventually wanted to get into films. One chap – no two of the chaps – said they were really writers but they had to pay the bills. Not the prats who stood in the sandwich queue at lunchtime using mobile phones. Bond salesmen playing Trivial Pursuit. But people who said they wanted to make a killing and then get out. We all had to wear red noses for Comic Relief and sponsor one of the partners for the marathon. One of the girls' boyfriends did sponsored abseiling. It was always someone's birthday or leaving party. There was always cake and champagne and grab bags full of bloody stupid presents and afterwards the trek to Covent Garden to get pissed in a tapas bar. I was glad.

David Of the elbow?

Christopher Yes. I was. It meant I didn't have to make a decision. I like cars.

David What's that?

Christopher It's a picture of a 1958 Buick convertible. Well I put up with your pictures. The statutory Matisse.

David You don't like anything. Except for cars. You don't.

Christopher I liked that play. That play.

David What play?

Christopher I liked it.

David What, that political play?

Christopher No, no. That play.

David I don't remember.

Christopher You do. That play.
  I want to set fire to him. I want to crash my bike into a moving lorry. Jump off the bridge. Throw him out of a moving taxi. Saved by the bell. Seconds out.
  I'm going up for the weekend.

David Oh, are you?

Christopher Yes. To see Jamie.

David This isn't your weekend.

Christopher I know.

David Oh.

Christopher I want to see if he's alright.

David He's alright.

Christopher She says not.

David I took him in didn't I? There's nothing wrong with him. Why does she think that a gluten free diet is the answer to an unhappy child? What's wrong with the child? He's got his imitation Royal Family coat. There's nothing wrong with him.

Christopher How do you know?

David I know.

Christopher You should know.

David I'm not a paediatrician. I'm an obstetrician. I was a paediatrician, briefly.

Christopher I thought you were a gynaecologist.

David I am.

Christopher Of course you think that no woman can give birth without you.

David I do sometimes. And sometimes I hear fathers at parties arrogate the birth of their children to themselves. We were in labour for 32 hours. We didn't properly dilate. We had a section.

Christopher Oh shouldn't fathers be at the birth of their own child?

David Yes, but it's got bugger all to do with the baby. It's a sort of narcissism. There are still women who don't want, can't have the man with them. They don't have someone holding their hands singing Ten Green Bottles. I want to say yes, you can be part of this if you promise to be with the child and its mother in ten years' time.

Christopher How's that woman?

David What woman?

Christopher What woman? All the other women you call cases or patients. This one has a name.

David Women do have names. They have names even if one doesn't know them. Even if you don't use them they have names.

21

Christopher Alright. How is she?

David Who? Mrs Murray?

Christopher Yes. She's the only one you ever talk about.

David She's back in.

Christopher Again. Why?

David Oh. To be safe. She brought me in a cake.

Christopher Do women still make cakes?

David Mrs Murray does.

Christopher What is it?

David Chocolate.

Christopher Great. Where is it?

David I had to leave it in the ward. I had to.

Christopher Didn't you bring a piece home?

David Perhaps there'll be some left tomorrow.

Christopher She wants to send him away to school.

David Where?

Christopher That school for very gifted parents. Christ knows who's going to pay. That'll be the next thing.

David Who's going to pay?

Christopher I'm not going to pay. I can't pay. He can go to a school locally like everyone else.

David You mean like you and me. She is his mother.

Christopher I know. I know.

David Well she is.

Christopher I know.

David She just is Christopher. Why don't you go back to her?

Christopher What? Why don't I go back to her? She's hard, she's mad, she's stupid, she's narrow, she's an impossibly selfish, materialistic, unlikeable, unkind, spurious . . . Oh forget it. Why don't I go back to her? She wouldn't have me.

David Do you want to fuck her?

Christopher Yeah I'd fuck her. Well you asked.

David You didn't have to say.

Christopher What does it matter?

David You know it does.

Christopher Oh . . .

David You know it does Christopher.

Christopher What is this, are we supposed to behave like some couple now are we?

David Yes.

Christopher You're giving me power. I don't want power.

David You don't want power? You want the power you want not the power I give you that's what you want.

Christopher I'm serious. Why must I be serious when you want to be serious.

David I think I taught you to be serious.

Christopher You want to dominate me dominating you.

David When?

Christopher When you take it out so you can see me see me come in your mouth.

23

David I somebody once but this nothing with evidence of his once assertive potential but now nothing as far as I'm concerned. He's as empty as he was but I can't get any pleasure of . . . Light up like a child. Illuminating . . . That I made light up. His light. Now nothing most off anyway. This for that and yes I was . . . if . . . of the . . . Then so intelligent.

Christopher You don't like me. You don't. You only fancy me because you think I'm straight. You were only interested in me because I was married. I think you think – no I think you want me to be shagging half London.

David The thing is when I go for a test each month it's only in case you've been fucking around since last month.

Christopher What?

David I always know or if not know in retrospect I realise I have known. If it was me I'd know how to deceive me without you even knowing. You're so selfish you can't even deceive successfully. You really don't want to deceive – you sort of don't mind if someone finds out. You're just careless.

Christopher Once.

David Once. What about? And.

Christopher Yeah alright.

David Bareback.

Christopher No.

David You can't even call her by her name.

Christopher It's you who won't use her name.

David I can't use her name if you won't. It's you who won't call her by her name.

Sometimes when I'm in the clinic you come into my mind with your not as thick as you think dick and I would really like to put your legs in the stirrup and say there there and fit you up.

For you I am someone to have laughs and be free with.

Christopher Yes.

David And free of.

Christopher You're going to make me want to go you know. I don't want to go but you are on your way you are to making me want to leave. You want me to go.

David Above me with that intent fag in the mouth don't disturb me I've got to get this wheel changed it will take some time man at work look. Your fag in the mouth hang on I've got to get this fixed air.

They talk now a lot about the addictive personality. They sometimes . . . They forget people who are spell-bound. Addicts under a spell. You are spellbinding and I am under your spell.

Christopher I feel I am letting you down in some way. I don't mean to let you down.

David When are you going?

Christopher Not now.

David Oh not now. When not now?

Christopher Don't let's – not now.

David Well I'm going to bed. I've got to be on duty for 72 hours.

Christopher Well that's fine and fucking dandy.

You're just trying . . . me . . . You're not even trying to make me. You're so . . . in a state you'll do anything for . . . Get out of my head. Get out of it. I'm . . . in and out of you. You . . . I feel I'm driving up the motorway the wrong way.

David What is it?

Christopher It's you when you're so desperate.

David I'm going to bed.
  You did look nice in a punt.

THREE

Michael and Stewart.

Michael I didn't think you'd ring.

Stewart I said I'd ring you.

Michael I know you did. I still didn't think you would. Why should you? I wouldn't have.

Stewart Well there's the difference between us isn't it? I wouldn't have said I would ring if I wasn't going to ring.

Michael You didn't say much on the phone.

Stewart Wasn't much to say.

Michael You came round quick enough.

Stewart I didn't.

Michael Oh.

Stewart I took my time. Anyway what's it matter? I wanted to come round.

Michael Good then, you're here.

Stewart Yeah that's right. Well then.

Michael What.

Stewart Come here.

He makes a move towards Michael.

Michael No.

Michael moves away.

Stewart Suit yourself. I can take my time.

He looks down at a pile of books on the floor

You still got all these books then.

Michael Yeah.

Stewart picks up a copy of 'The Gift Relationship' by R. H. Titmuss.

Stewart 'The Gift Relationship.' 'From human blood to social policy.' When was that written? When the world was young? What have you been doing with yourself?

Michael Do you mean today?

Stewart Today, yesterday. What's the matter with you? Do you want me to go? I'm not going.

Michael Or it could be . . .

Stewart I'm gasping for a fag. D'you smoke?

Michael I don't. I'm sorry. I know, let's go and get some. Why don't you go and get some?

Stewart I'm skint.

Michael I've got money.

Stewart Let's go for a drink then.

Michael Oh.

Stewart Yeah! C'mon.

Michael OK.

Stewart D'you play pool? I'll teach you to play pool.

Michael I can play pool.

Stewart You can't play pool. Can you play pool?

Michael Of course. Can you?

Stewart Of course. I'm brilliant. I've kept myself in fags playing pool.

Michael Or it could be . . .
What is it?

   Stewart is rubbing his eye.

Stewart I think I've got something in my eye.

Michael Come here.

Stewart No.

Michael Pull your lid over it.

Stewart No.

Michael Go on.

   Stewart does so.

Now how is it?

Stewart I think it's better. Thanks. No it's still here.

Michael Come here. Come here.

Stewart No.

Michael Come on. Hold still.

   He removes the grit from Stewart's eye.

There we are, look. There we are. OK?

Stewart Thanks.

Michael Or . . .
  Can you whistle?

Stewart Course I can whistle.

Michael You know, like this. Can you whistle like this?

  With his fingers in his mouth, Michael makes a loud whistle.

Stewart Of course I can.

Michael Go on then.

  Stewart attempts and fails.

Michael I thought you couldn't.

Stewart What does that mean?

Michael Or . . .

Stewart How are you?

Michael Good, very good.

Stewart Good.

Michael I wish you hadn't asked that.

Stewart Why?

Michael Now I don't feel so good. I felt fine, now I feel fairly fucking terrible.
  Or . . .
  What if he keeps his cigarettes in his teeshirt? Oh my God.
  Or . . .

Stewart I came down two years ago.

Michael Or . . .
  More brutal exchanges don't you think? Regardless of my views on the matter.
  Or . . .

Stewart I'm not living anywhere special.

Michael Or . . .
  Sometimes I think I'm as intelligent as I pretend to be.
  Or . . .

  They sit on the floor to talk.

Stewart I came down with this young lassie. We travelled down together. After I got picked up by the police, she went back. I was bevvying a bit. No money. No kip. I was sent down. You couldn't blame her.

Michael Or . . .

Stewart I was in this doss in London and one morning I went to take a piss, and someone came in and said where's Lenny and tried to kick the cubicle door in. So I went into the next cubicle and I pulled myself up to look about, and there he was, Lenny, sitting with his head rolled back and a needle beside him on the floor. Then the superintendent rang the police and said he's dead as far as I can see. Take your time anyway. He's no use to anyone. An old man died in the same doss, so the authorities came to take the body away. They handed him as far as the landing and one of them says 'hey up' to the men below and tipped him over the banister. They never caught him. They put him in a box and carted him off.

Michael Or . . .

  They roll towards each other simultaneously, one tumbling over the other as they meet and end up some distance apart, each lying on his back.

Stewart I like being with you. I do. D'you hear me? You. What about you. Hey.

He hurls a book at Michael.

Michael You're beautiful. I know that.

FOUR

Tony sitting. Andrew comes in.

Andrew I'm sorry.

Tony S'alright. Sit down.

Andrew You fed the dog?

Tony Yes.

Andrew You taken him out?

Calls the dog

Tony I have. Leave him. Sit down.

Andrew I'm sorry. I'm late.

Tony Do you want your tea?

Andrew No. I'm alright. You had your tea?

Tony No. I'm having something later.

Andrew I'll make you something.

Tony No. I'll have a cup of tea.

Andrew Yeah. I'll have a cup of tea.
Why haven't you asked me why I'm late?

Tony You'll tell me. I don't have to ask you.

Andrew Why don't you ask me? Don't you want to know? You angry?

Tony No. Why should I be angry? You're not very late.

Andrew Sure you're not hungry?

Tony No I'm not. I'm not angry either.

Andrew Do you want to go out later?

Tony No. Get in first. What do you want to go out for? You only just come in.

Andrew Alright. Keep your hair on. We'll stay in. I don't want go out. We'll stay in. You'll read the paper. I'll watch the telly. I'll read the paper and you'll watch the telly and then we both might watch the telly.

Tony That's right.

Andrew And you won't say anything.

Tony That's right.

Andrew All night.

Tony That's right. I'll listen you you.
   Don't you want stay in?

Andrew Yeah. I'll make us something to eat later on.

Tony No. I'll do that. Sit down love.

Andrew Why don't you want to know why I'm so late? I might have been out for a drink with someone.

Tony You might have. But you haven't.

Andrew I might have had an assignation.

Tony Might you.

Andrew I might have.

Tony Don't.

Andrew With –

Tony Don't.

Andrew See. You don't know. Do you?

Tony Who?

Andrew No one.

Tony Who?

Andrew No one. No one.

Tony That . . . In the showroom.

Andrew Sh. Don't sulk. Give us a kiss then. Come on. No one.

Kisses him.

Tony Be quiet now, for fuck's sake. And have a cup of tea. What's the matter with you? You never used to be like this.

Andrew Like what?

Tony I don't know. Oh all the time asking questions. Why don't you take the dog out?

Andrew No. I used to be docile. Like your mother. Not any more. Not me.

Tony Leave my mum out of it.

Andrew Yes, sonny. No, sonny. Ooh.

Tony Leave it out.
I spoke to her today. She asked how you were.

Andrew She sympathises with me. You're spoilt. She spoilt you.

Tony She did. I am.

Andrew See. Well, I'm not your mother. Not any more, I'm not.

Tony I think among the most stupid things, one of the most stupid things, no, the most stupid, stupid thing, stupid, is to say I'm not your mother.

Andrew Well, I'm not. So don't blame me, and don't start.

Tony For what?

Andrew For not being your mother. Because, I'm not.

Tony I don't want you to be my mother, what you talking about.

Andrew Good. Because I'm not. Going to sulk now. You can't have a conversation.

Tony I can have a conversation. I don't want a conversation. You pretend you want a conversation. You don't want a conversation. What's the matter with you?

Andrew I don't know. I don't know what's the matter with me.

Do you know what they're talking about?

Tony Who?

Andrew The papers, the radio, the telly.

Points to the newspaper.

Here, this. I really don't know what they're talking about half the time. The chosen. Men. Decisions. I really don't.

Tony Who?

Andrew Men. To be a man, you see, you've got to be a clown. You've got to be able to act the fool. I can't act the fool. I can't clown about.

What are we doing together?

Tony Oh don't. What's the matter with you? Not a man. Where you been then?

Andrew Nowhere. I been round Robert's. Nowhere.

Tony Well then, that's it. He's wound you up.

Andrew He's alright.

Tony You come back like this.

Andrew Like what? I can go round there.

Tony Yeah.

Andrew You jealous?

Tony Of him? Get real.

Andrew Why haven't you come out to your mother?

Tony You see, that's him, that is. It's always the same. He winds you up. Why haven't you come out to your mother? Shut up. Shut up.

Andrew I didn't come out to my mother because I didn't want to give her the pleasure of it. I don't want to give her the opportunity of expressing whatever it is she'd want to express. Either way. Give her the chance. But your mother likes you. She worships you.

Tony Your mother likes you.

Andrew No. She doesn't. It doesn't matter. It's your father you're afraid of.

Tony I don't want to come out to no one.

Andrew But you could come out to your mum.

Tony This is all. Shut up. All this is. What are sexual politics? Talking about it. Analysing it. It was his idea to get a gay plumber. Gay plumber. Who wanted a gay plumber?

Andrew I didn't want a gay plumber.

Tony You did. We did.

Andrew I thought we should show solidarity.

Tony Yes. Well.

Andrew No. I don't want. Don't. Don't come that with me. I don't want all this . . . gay. Gay this, gay that. I thought it would be a good idea to have a gay plumber. See. Well people are. Blokes are discriminated against.

Tony You're giving importance to what we can't do fuck all about. Let's just keep calm. What's the matter with you tonight? I get upset about what normal people get upset about. What I know about fox hunting? I don't give a toss about fox hunting. See. You get it all out of kilter.

Andrew I can't have views?

Tony That's not what I mean. Yes. But you said what we doing together. You said that last night. I said, talk like you won't be together with no one. Shut up. Let's get on with it. Don't think. Think. Think. You're no better a thinker than what I am. I want to get on with it. You'd be a bundle of laughs in the back of the pictures, you would. You'd be a bundle of laughs in the back of a parked car.

Andrew You can't say it. You never say it.

Tony I don't want to say it.

Andrew I don't want to say it. I do say it though. On Valentine's Day, who bought you a praline heart? I wasn't intending to.

Tony Yes.

Andrew You ate it though, didn't you? You don't believe in it, you say it's silly. It don't mean anything. I would. I would do what you want.

Tony What is it you want? What? You've tied me up in some difficult knots.

Andrew I haven't. It's you. You won't shift.

Tony I don't wanna shift.

Andrew You won't beat me. You won't.

Tony I'm not trying to. What you talking about? Don't laugh.

They laugh.

Andrew This . . . Parallelism. The parallel lines of this. On the parallel. We'll never meet. I don't want any more. Yes. Like it was yesterday.

Tony What?

Andrew And today. This morning. I don't want any more. Just don't make it worse.

Tony Make what worse? I don't get, I don't get, I don't, I don't get it.

Andrew It's me. It's me.

Tony What's you?

Andrew I'm not a man. I'm not a leader. I'm not a man. I'm letting my sister do everything. Sort out whether my mother should go into a home. I'm not serious.

Tony What . . . How . . . you not serious?

Andrew Well, listen. No listen. For a start, to start with, men without children aren't serious.

Tony Don't talk about kids. That's all nothing to do with me alright? That's not my concern. What do you want to concern yourself with that for?

Andrew Why can't you talk about anything?

Tony What's this to talk about?

Andrew I wasn't asking anything. I only perhaps wanted to talk about it. I only wanted to talk about what just crossed my mind. I don't think I could bring up a kid.

I realise I hate my mother entirely. Still see that friend of yours, what's his name? It's the victims, the victims I think about. That's my mother. Yeah. 'You don't want to do that.' But mum, I've lived. I've jumped over the fence. 'That's nice then.' I'm not serious.

Tony Look. I don't want to talk about this. I don't want to be a woman. I don't want to talk about it. Grow up. We're not special. This isn't a marriage.

Andrew I know that doesn't mean you don't have to work at it.

Tony You can't let go – can you? Can you though? You won't let it happen between us. There's all the outside, you've got to bring it home. I'm tired of all the outside. And there's plenty to talk about. You take seriously what's yours to be talked about. There's nothing more important than you and me. There's no more. We're not going through all that. That opinion. How we going through it. That. All that. It's not happening to us. It's not what's happening to us.

Andrew But it is happening to us. I'm trying to make it happen see. I don't want no more silent nights.

Tony I don't know what you're talking about.

Andrew You do.

Tony Nah. Don't know. I'm afraid I don't know. I don't know anything about it. I don't know nothing, I'm ignorant, me. Where's the paper gone?

Andrew You do.

He crumples up the paper.

Tony Don't do that to the paper. Fuck. I'll fist you. Fuck it. I'll do you.
    What's the matter? Isn't it alright? Here with me.

Andrew Yes. No. Of course it is.

Tony And it's better out there.

Andrew No. I don't know.

Tony No.

Andrew Not the wine bar stuff. Not stuff your face. Hang out, chill out. Clubbing. Football. Go for a run. Go to the gym. Do weights. Oh, I'm in computers, me. Chemical engineering. Oh me, I work in a sports centre. Rented cars, insurance, rental, the retail business. Booking office, quality control, maintenance office, record shop, men's tailoring, computer graphics. And explaining *this*. I'm living with my mate. In a side street, know it? Yes. Original features. Garden flat. Paved garden, music centre, deep freeze, rag rolled walls, uncover that fireplace. Star Trek books. Star Trek video. I don't want to miss Prisoner of Cell Block H. Flat! Investment. Who's paying the mortgage? Ooh. Nice.

Tony I'm paying the mortgage.

Andrew Yes. It's not even mine. Who am I?

Tony Well, you shouldn't worry. You'll get your mother's place, share it with your sister. Talk to her.

Andrew Let's go to a car boot sale. I like car boot sales.

Tony You do.

Andrew Look at this barbie. I got a soap dish. That's me. Plastic! Cool. Plastic toast rack. Look at this plate, that record. Tape for the car. Tape for the car. Annie Lennox. The Tourists.

Tony What's wrong with it?

Andrew That's not life. That's getting a life, that is. Get a life. Get a life. I don't want a life. Life happens between those things.

Tony That's life.
Sit down. Be quiet.

Andrew If I challenge you, you'll go away you will. If I go away, you'll get over it, you will. That's your mother, it is. If I stay, what'll I do? This for a little love.

Tony Not so bad.

Andrew When through all the thoughts I clear a path I think I'm alive. This is alright. This is OK. The light in the sky reflected as my eyes brim. Then this almost . . . feeling. I think of you. I have to love you. I know I must. It's as though I've been born. Or joy or something.

He makes to go out.

Tony Where you going?

Andrew Take the dog out. Judy, here dog.

FIVE

David and Christopher are drinking tea from mugs.

David Not herbal tea. Not herbal tea.

Christopher Yes herbal tea. It's quite nice.

David What's it made of?

Christopher I dunno.

David You don't know what it's made of.

Christopher Drink it.

David I can't drink this.

Christopher Well make a cup of tea then.

David You make better tea than me.

Christopher Yes.

David You do. You do Christopher.

Christopher Drink it.

David It's awful.

Christopher It's good for you. It won't make you so jumpy.

David What's it called?

Christopher Happy Apple.

David It doesn't taste very happy. Anything to eat?

Christopher Nothing.

David What else? There's bound to be something.

Christopher You want me to get you something?

David No thanks. I don't really want anything. I think I've got a temperature. Why did you buy this?

Christopher Just drink it David.

David You're always in a foul mood when you come back.

Christopher You're always in a foul mood when I come back.

David You're always in a foul mood when you take him back.

Christopher I'm not. I'm always a bit sad. Is that alright?

David Do you think I've got a temperature?

Christopher Nope.

David I think I have.

Christopher Here. Nope.

David Get the thermometer.

Christopher You haven't got a temperature. Shut it.

David Christ you're happy.

Christopher Right. Where's the thermometer?

He goes out.

David I rang you. I exist. When you're there I'm here OK.

Christopher comes back in with a thermometer.

Christopher Here. I'll put it in.

David Oh ay.

Christopher puts the thermometer in David's mouth.

Christopher I don't feel responsible – in any way. I look at him in wonder but I don't feel very proud of myself. Of him of him. Oh, of him.
Here.

He takes out the thermometer.

David It's not cooked.

Christopher Nothing see.

David I rang you.

Christopher Yes.

David I rang you. I exist. When you're there I'm here.

Christopher I know. She makes a thing about it. Silently.

David Oh really. You didn't ask me why I rang.

Christopher I know why you rang.

David To see how he was. What was the matter?

Christopher There was nothing the matter. As usual it was a false alarm. You told me so. That's not why you rang.

David No?

Christopher It's the same when she rings here.

David Where did you sleep?

Christopher Where do you think I slept?

David I don't know.

Christopher Look it's not as if I'm there very often.

David Did you like it?

Christopher It was quite pleasant. No it wasn't.

David What's up?

Christopher Nothing. What's the matter with you?

David Why are you allowing her to still have this effect on you? It makes me feel great.

Christopher I suppose I must feel something. I hate her so much. Say something David.

David She's not my kind of girl. She's too winsome. That hair. That Little Miss Muffet outfit. That juvenile miniskirt. You couldn't kill her with cyanide. Why are

43

you making me say all this? You know I don't like her. Girls like a fairy on a Christmas tree. It's not so much her as you. She must be alright. She's got a very nice child. At least I like him. Except she's got this thing about his skin, his teeth, the usual nonsense. Feeding him carrot – no chocolate. What about school?

Christopher Nothing about school. Digs about money.

David What was that nursery school he went to? The rat hole.

Christopher Squirrel Corner.

David It must be the only Montessori school in Hertfordshire. Is he coming next weekend, Jamie?

Christopher Yes. If that's alright.

David It's fine. He can watch me play cricket. What with you under a car and me at the crease, he's not short of healthy role models.

Christopher I feel bad about him. I don't feel responsible in any way. I look at him in wonder but I don't feel very proud of myself.

David Not of him?

Christopher Of him. Of him. Oh of him. Yes of him. What does he make of things?

David Well he knows.

Christopher How?

David Children know. Look don't worry. You wear pyjamas. He wears pyjamas. I wear pyjamas. He wears a dressing gown. You wear a dressing gown. I wear a dressing gown. All we need is Horlicks and a briar pipe. We could get my mother to embroider a Radio Times cover.

Christopher Your mother.

David What do you mean? You like my mother.

Christopher Your father.

David My father. Your father.

Christopher Oh my father. My mother thinks you're a nice boy. How's that woman?

David She's fine.

Christopher She still in?

David Yes. We're going to keep her in. Not long now.

Christopher She got a husband?

David I don't know. I think so. I suppose so.

Christopher Why do you like her?

David I don't know that I do. I think because she's angry.

Christopher Why does she like you? They all like you.

David But she likes me for my mind.

Christopher What's wrong with her?

David Nothing actually wrong with her – but she's had four children – all difficult pregnancies. She's going to name the baby after me.

Christopher I found a letter.

David Where?

Christopher In her sewing table.

David Does she sew?

Christopher Not much but she sews. It was her grand-mother's. That's where she keeps her letters. Ones she wants to keep.

David For others to read. What was in it?

Christopher There were quite a few. I knew she'd been seeing someone.

David How did you know?

Christopher I knew. And from what Jamie said. Ages ago. He stays quite frequently it seems.

David You didn't say.

Christopher I'm saying now.

David Who is it?

Christopher An old boyfriend. A friend of her brother's. They're well suited.

David Christ.

Christopher There was nothing about me in the letters.

David Should there be?

Christopher He's a creep. A real creep. He wears his hair in a ponytail.

David What does he do?

Christopher Nothing. This and that. He's got a bookshop and he's split up from his wife and he's got two children – one of them's called Merlin. And he's part of some New Age community and he's given her these crystals. He's healing Jamie's allergy with them.

David Jamie doesn't have an allergy.

Christopher Jamie told me they'd been to a vigil – a candlelit vigil. What can I do?

David Absolutely nothing. I'll have to have a paracetomol. Have we got any?

Christopher What do you want a paracetomol for? I don't know if we've got any.

David I can't have a temperature.

Christopher You haven't got a temperature. Stay there. I'll get you one.

SIX

Michael and Stewart.
  Michael sits by Stewart.

Michael Can't you get a job?

Stewart I don't want a job. I've had a job.

Michael I'm sorry. I'm sorry.

  Michael gradually moves towards Stewart on his hands and knees but stops before reaching him.

Stewart That's OK.

Michael I just meant. Well.

Stewart What?

Michael You seem.

Stewart What?

Michael I don't know. You're . . . Oh . . . Money . . . You're so . . . I want. Oh . . . Are you OK?

Stewart I'm OK. The giro'll do for me. I've had jobs.

Michael Or . . .
  What is it?

Stewart Nothing.

Michael You can tell me.

Stewart Nothing. I'm alright.

Michael Or . . .

Stands.

You're a lazy fucker.

Stewart Well you'd know.

Stands.

Michael You take the action for the deed, that's your trouble.
Or . . .

Stewart Look, Lenny was already on it. I don't do smack or anything much. I can take it or leave it. I'd rather a drink which is just as well on my income. What business is it of yours anyway?

Michael Or . . .

Stewart Look.

He shows Michael his hand.

Michael What?

Stewart Sweating.

Michael That's alright.

Stewart No it isn't. I don't like it.

Michael Come here.

He takes Stewart's hand and licks it.

Stewart You . . .

Stewart makes a fist at him, joking.

Michael Or it could be . . .
Then it could be . . .

Or it could be . . .

Stewart Do you want me to stay?

Michael Or it could be . . . No.
Or . . . No.

Stewart What's the matter?

Michael Or . . .

Stewart What is it?

Michael Or . . . No.
Or . . .

Stewart It's alright.

He tries to comfort Michael.

Michael No.

Michael pushes him away.

Stewart Come on. Come on. What's the matter?

Stewart persists.

Michael No.

Michael pushes him away.

Stewart Come on.

Michael No.

He pushes Stewart away, violently.

Stewart What is it? What is it?

Michael How am I going to get through? A lot of people spend their lives just in drink . . . When you drop dead. Do you want everlasting life? Just to grow old when you come to think of it. Does that worry you? I think the problems start when you start listening to yourself.

I know who I am but I don't know where I am. I'm all over the fucking place. This is awful. I could . . . Go away. I have to be by myself. If I could put myself in touch with my feelings I'd probably kill you. It's when you're not here I want you. I want to reach across and hold on to you. To hold you. Only I seem not to be allowed any feelings. I seem not to have feelings except sentimental ones. Or I seem only to have feelings. I seem to be all feelings.

Michael rejects Stewart again.

Don't please. I'm frightened, I'm OK. I walk around and even now when I'm talking . . . If someone had died I'd have some reason for this. I'd have some right to this feeling. If you died. If someone had just died even. If you were dead. But I haven't first call. You see . . . I think . . . You see to dwell upon the ulterior motive for the sake of truth is . . . To overemphasise that everything is dependant upon motive. To emphasise *that* truth is to deny that ulterior motive does not only produce results for the self. To think altruism is only worth measuring by ulterior motive is wrong. Stupid. Or to deny spontaneity. I'll have to get it together. How am I going to get it together?

Stewart You will.

Michael Do you think so?

Stewart You will.

Michael Never mind. I'm in pieces. Not even pieces, scraps. I'll have to get it together. How am I going to get it together?

Stewart You will.

Stewart embraces him.

Michael Do you think so? I don't think I ever will.

Stewart You will.

Michael moves away.

Michael Yet there's another part of me that doesn't give a fuck.

SEVEN

Andrew and Robert.

Robert Did you walk into a door?

Andrew Yeah. Something like that.

Robert How did you do it?

Andrew I could fucking kill him. I could fucking punch him. I could punch hell out of him. Cheek. I'm really mad.

Robert Sit.

Andrew No, I'm too . . . I am. I'm fucking mad at this. No. I can't. I'm sorry.

Robert What you going to do?

Andrew I'm going to kill him. I'm going to fucking kill him. I'm going to break everything up. Smash all the windows and then when he loses his temper again. Then in that case I'll knife him. Or poison the dog.

Robert Apart from that, what are you going to do? Here.

Gives him a drink.

Andrew Thanks.

Drinks.

Christ. I don't know. He went. He fancies himself.
I should have knocked him out. I'm furious.

Robert Why didn't you?

Andrew I could have. I could have, I could. I could have
him. He thinks he's mister . . . He's stupid, I wouldn't
give him the pleasure. I should have, what's this now?
Domestic violence. Abuse. What are two grown men
doing living together faking all the stupidities of a fake
straight relationship, what's all that about?

Robert Ah well. What's all that about. If we only knew
what that's all about. Sex. That's what it's usually about.

Andrew No. No, it's not sex. No. I don't want to talk
about that. I don't think you should.
    There's something wrong about the whole thing.

Robert What?

Andrew Everything. Everything. I don't want to be an
imitation of an imitation.

Robert Of what?

Andrew Of everything. Yeah. Everything. Gay pride.
Gay shame, that's what this is. No everything. The thing
I'm copying. I don't want it or what it stands for. It's a
form of what my mother wants.
    Did you go to Diana's funeral?

Robert Yes. I thought I should.

Andrew I didn't. That's what I mean. I don't know what
it is. But I don't want it. No. Don't laugh.
    What's gay culture?

Robert What's gay culture?

52

Andrew What underpants you got on?

Robert Yes, well . . .

Andrew Calvins.

Robert Yes.

Andrew That's gay culture. That's about the size of it. Don't laugh. The make of your underpants.

Robert Oh I don't . . .

Andrew Well what else. What else has come out of gay culture? Discos. Body fascism. Is there a gay community?

Robert Well in so far as gay men oppress themselves, there's very like what you call a gay community. I can't imagine there's been much of a call for a homeland though. I don't think we need one. Queers we will always have with us. But you're searching for a solution. What if there is no solution to anything.

Andrew I'll just have to go on looking.

Robert Have you ever been to Pride?

Andrew No. I wanted to go. He wouldn't, see. To see what it's like.

Robert Well you should go the once. I only went the once. But it's not me. But then neither is the Last Night of the Proms. So you can't go by me. I wouldn't like the Highland Games. Or the County Show. Or the Welsh National Eisteddfod. Or St Patrick's Day in New York. Or an Orange March. Or the Notting Hill Carnival. Or Badminton or the Cup Final.

I'm not a great fan of the British Legion.

. . . But being queer can be a project like anything else. It's not your particular project. We all have our axes to grind. Why shouldn't being queer be an axe to grind like other people's? It's not something it's easy to avoid. Some people try.

Andrew Well you don't grind the queer axe.

Robert I hope I do in my own way. It's whether you believe in a continuum or categorical differences. For all the apparent freedom these are prescriptive times. There are choices and they want you to make them. For some you've got to wear a suit or at least a jacket. Have what they call a partner. Now there's a word. There's a word for the market place.

Andrew I don't want to have a partner. It makes you sound like a firm.

Robert I think that's the idea. Makes you into a sound financial proposition.

Andrew I doubt if anyone without an income has a partner.

Robert Settle down. Get a mortgage. Join the Rotary Club. Join the party. Take part. It's the price you have to pay for being comfortable.

Andrew I don't want to take part.

Robert Well join the radical wing of the movement. Where to be really queer you have to have someone nail your foreskin to a piece of wood and generally kick up a fuss. All this sounds much better in the original French. It loses a lot in the translation. Transgressive. Now there's a word too. I have a sneaking sympathy for all this. I think queers are still ultimately transgressive. Jouissance. The unkennelled seeking out of the difference. But in English it all takes on a homely air. The transgressors always turn out to sound like George Formby. The rank smell of poppers and leathers and the seeking for jouissance in the wilds of the heath and I'll thank you to keep a civil tongue up my arse. Hoping to star in a cluster fuck but settling for just being Mrs Norman Maine. I don't think that's for you. Nor the New Labour Old Comptom Street cool Brittania queens. The all inclusive, one price, fun and funky, up for nothing, body conscious, size queens. Disco dollies who think you're old at 27. Cock-led love, cock-led lives. Unaffectionate, meretricious, coarse, conventional. I'd rather the Judy queens. They can at least talk about something. The people I'm talking about haven't got the attention span to take in a drag act. Can't you see the funny side of it?

Andrew Only too fucking well.

Robert That's the mainstream. We're just another niche in the market. And that suits everyone down to the ground. Well able and willing to be neutralised. Sentimental, silly, frivolous, a bit of a laugh, very sympathetic listeners, harmless fodder for gay nights on TV. A convenient addition to popular culture, for the whim of TV executives. Part of the dumbing down. Manipulated by people who having had considerable cultural advantages themselves, want to deny it to others because they're too lazy and too greedy to do otherwise. I don't think there is a gay sensibility. Not a stable one. This all part of the straight man's game.

The success of Judy Garland or Barbra Streisand or Maria Callas can't have been decided on by gay men. Or Stephen Sondheim. Even. Even. There have always been straight queens. We're part of their entertainment. It's to do with a struggle that everyone has with the fact of gender. The anger of all of us at being biologically sorted. Look at straight men. Most straight men are male impersonators. We're making a fuss. Look at the fuss they make in the confusion. But all the while for us and our African brothers and sisters there's something that cracks the whole thing open. The demand for viral rights by that little unsentient claimant to life. That undermines the whole show. You want to know why you're with someone. Don't think there's much more to it than knowing who you're spending the weekend with or Easter or Bank Holidays. It's someone to share the torture with.

What's the alternative? That's what most people have concluded. Gay men aren't different from anyone else in that respect. People aren't in couples for the general good. I don't see pair bonding as some predetermined absolute. We're all much the same. Except that women are seen to be more mysterious than men, more inscrutable. Men are quite straightforward. Their selfishness is so entirely predictable.

Andrew But what about people who haven't got a partner?

Robert Or lost one.

Andrew I'm sorry.

Robert Well what are you going to do?

Andrew I don't know.
No it's not my feeling for him that's fake. I don't think. It's something else. If I don't see him it will be alright but I dread the sense of worthlessness at the prospect. I'm so angry. I'm so frightened. I'll collapse. Where's my inhaler? He's so vain. I like vain men. I like a bit of vanity.

Robert You fool. You don't want to put up with it. He done it before?

Andrew Threatened.

Robert I'm worried now.

Andrew He takes a liberty with a privilege. He wouldn't do it again in a hurry. I don't care if it's my fault. It probably is. He'll have to learn to punch the wall.

Robert When did it happen?

Andrew Last night. I went round my sister's. He's been trying to phone me. He been here? He'd be too scared.

Robert What your sister say?

Andrew She didn't say anything. She says her husband doesn't understand her.

Robert What did you do?

Andrew The dark hours went and I got some sleep. I haven't been to work.

Tony comes in.

Tony You're here then.

Andrew Yeah I am. That's right.

Tony I didn't know.

Andrew No you didn't.

Robert Do you want anything to drink?

Tony Yeah. No I'm alright. Honest. Thank you. Thank you. You coming home?

Andrew No, I'm not.

Tony The dog misses you.

Andrew Yeah. Look I'm going.

Tony Don't go.

Andrew Yeah. Thanks. I'm off.

Robert You sure?

Andrew Yeah. Tara. Tara.
  I'll see you.

Tony Why you going?

Andrew So long.

He goes.

Robert Let him go.

Tony Did he tell what happened?

Robert Not really.

Tony Oh dear. Stupid. I wish it hadn't happened. You know. I don't know what to do now. What do you think?

Robert I don't know.

Tony When I first knew him it was before you knew him.

Robert Yeah.

Tony Yeah.

Robert What does that mean?

Tony Nothing.
    He didn't know anything. He just was, I don't know, innocent. That's it. Even naive. He didn't know anything about sex. Nothing. That was so sexy about him. He's a little bit Country, I'm a little bit Rock and Roll.
    Please don't.

Robert What?

Tony Please don't take him from me.

Robert No.

Tony You're going to take him from me.

Robert I'm not. I'm not. What makes you think. I'm not interested in him.

Tony Please don't tell him I've spoken to you. Will you?

Robert Of course not. Come on.

Tony I'm horny.

Robert Are you? Come on.

Tony Sorry. Thanks. Thank you.
Last night. I came round here. Was he here?

Robert No. He wasn't here.

Tony Where was he?

Robert I don't know. You'll have to ask him.

Tony I was outside here. It was damp in the street.

Robert Why didn't you ring the bell?

Tony No. No I just pulled my coat collar up and watched till the lights went out. Till there was one on in the bedroom.

EIGHT

Andrew and Terry.

Terry No. I like old men. I wanna be old. I can't wait.
I went into care first when I was three. In and out, you know. Then I got out of control. I never went to school. I never went to school, never. Honest. I didn't. I used to nick my mother's fags for her, mate. They were my family, they was all criminals. Thieves. They weren't honest.
My father's family. My father. We don't know where he came from. Not Roehampton. He lives in America now. They was very unaffectionate. I just used to thieve for my mum. I can't go there now. My uncle died. My grandmother wouldn't have me in the flat. She says I'm the worst. I went to boarding school. I did. The masters was OK. It was the older boys, that's what it was.

Eighteen-year-olds and that. Abuse, like. I used to get in bed with my mate. Then, like, you're sixteen. You're not in care, are you? Anyway. Out. Off you go.

I like you. I like your voice. Posh. Like your eyes. Your mouth. Look see. Gold filling. I'd like a gold tooth.

Andrew Where you living?

Terry I'm staying with my mate, the other block from my grandmother. I keep out of her way. It's cool.

I'd like to keep lizards. Cold blooded. No I like the feel of them. Cold blooded. I like really scary books. Stephen King. Have you ever read a book by Edgar Allan Poe?

Andrew Do you like girls?

Terry Girls. Yeah, I like girls. Girls all are OK. Aren't they. No. I'm like, well, you fuck a girl easier, like. Obvious. But blokes suck cock better, don't they? Funny that, innit? They're more, like, industrious. Hungry. Not greedy. They go for it. I like blokes. I know more about geezers. Girls are all over you. I've always been round blokes. Most of the girls I know wear knickers to keep, their ankles warm. No. That's not right. I like some girls. I know a girl I like. But she's chirping all the time. Giving it this. Some lyrics don't half come out of her mouth, honest.

What's this then, where you live?

Andrew My mother's flat.

Terry She in?

Andrew No, no. She's in a home.

Terry Oh yeah.
This yours?

Andrew No. My sister wants to sell. But I don't think we can. I don't think it'd be right. She might come back.

60

Terry You always lived here?

Andrew No I only been here. I left . . . You know, I told you.

Terry Oh, him. You wanna kick him to the kerb mate. He's a dog. You want me in here. Look after you. Get the shopping and that. What's the matter? OK?

Andrew Yeah.

Terry You alright?
  You're trying to make me queer, I think. You trying to make me queer. I think you are.

  He pulls up his sleeve.

Andrew What's that?

  He takes hold of his arm.

Terry No.

Andrew I'm sorry.

Terry No. It's alright. Look.

Andrew What's that? Needle marks.

Terry What? You seen needle marks in ridges like that?

Andrew I'm sorry.

Terry I used to cut myself. Nah. It's alright. I never do it now. See – these are old. I don't do it now.

Andrew What you do it with?

Terry Anything what cuts. Razor blades. It's. Oh well.

Andrew Why?

Terry Why. Well, like they said it's only to get attention. It's . . . no, I can't. I can't explain it. I don't do it no more. I ain't a kid like that no more. No I got more sense now.

Andrew Why you looking at me like that?

Terry Because that's how you was looking at me son earlier.

Andrew Was I?

Terry Yeah. You was. You're cute, ain't you. Come on.

Andrew I always want it to be over. It's the chase, you know. As much as doing it, isn't it? As much as the act.

Terry What? What you talking about?

Andrew No, it's alright.

Terry Well what we gonna do?

Andrew I don't know.

Terry Well suck my cock then. Do you want to? Suck me off then. OK.

Andrew Blimey.

Terry See. You love it. You been a naughty boy.

Andrew You got anything on you?

Terry I haven't got anything. I haven't brought anything on purpose. Live dangerous.

Andrew No then.

Terry Come, you want it. I want it. You want to feel the tip of my cock nuzzling in your arse, don't you? You do.

Andrew Not safe.

Terry Don't be soft. If it's going to get you, it's going to get you. Next time I'll bring loads of condoms.

Andrew No.

Terry I like meeting people like you. You're interesting. I like talking to you. You're good, you are.

You got something to drink?

Andrew No. Tea.

Terry No. Yeah. No, hurry.

Well, what we gonna do?

No. I come down there with my friends. We saw all these geezers hanging about. What was we on? We was on something.

Andrew Oh yeah.

Terry No. I was just walking through there tonight. No. Leave it out.

Andrew Do you want anything?

Terry What?

Andrew Do you need anything, you know. Do you?

Terry No, I don't want money. I don't want your money. No. I don't do nothing for money. No. You can give us a fag, you got one?

Andrew Yeah. Yeah. Yeah. Of course. Do you want them?

Terry What?

Andrew Do you want a keep them?

Terry Thanks mate. Sweet. I ain't got any indoors. I'll have a couple, OK? No I don't want money though. You know I only ever done one bad thing like that, yeah?

Andrew What's that?

Terry Well like I met this bloke and, like I said, like, I'd see him again, you know. And of course I lose his number, right. Straight up. Of course. And then I then

I didn't go round there and that. Well, one day, my mate, I owed this bloke money and he had to have it and I was skint. I said to him 'I can't – I ain't got a lot of money.' I'll see you the weekend. And he had to have it, you know. He really did. I had no money nowhere. So I was near his house. The bloke. I thought, oh well. So I rang on my mobile. You got a mobile?

Andrew Yes.

Terry Excellent. You got a pager?

Andrew No. I thought you lost his number?

Terry No. I had, it was on a bit of paper in this jacket. This jacket I was wearing, straight, and he was in. I said, like, if I come would he pay for the cab. Couldn't think of anything else. And it was OK.

Andrew Why didn't you just ask him for money?

Terry No. I couldn't. I couldn't. Honest, I couldn't. So he give money for the cab at the door and I took it and I never went back. That's bad, that's bad, that is. Like a junkie, like, or something, innit. I don't like that. I should give it back. I'm going go over there one day. I am. I know where he lives.

Andrew What did you used to do

Terry What did I do? Thieving. Houses. You . . . Someone says, you know, know where I can get a radio? I don't do it no more.

Andrew You sign on?

Terry Sign on? No. They can keep it. They don't worry me. Them.

Andrew What would you like to do?

Terry What would I like to do? Nothing. What could I be?

Andrew Lots of things.

Terry I could be a TV chef. I like cooking. Or have a chat show – like Montel. Or I could be in a boy band. Yeah.

Andrew Would you steal round here?

Terry Them flats? I would. They can afford it. I wouldn't do something like here. No they wouldn't miss it. I don't do that now. I don't want to go inside again.

Andrew No you don't.

Terry No. I don't. You're right, I know – I shouldn't. Too fucking true. I'm keeping out of it. Oh yeah. I'm sure. I'm not doing that any more. Ain't worth it. As it is they pick on you for anything once they know you, mate. It's worse in prison.

No you can't cure paedophiles, mate. Not if you castrated them, you wouldn't.

Andrew What can you do then?

Terry You'd have to kill 'em, you wanna cure 'em. They don't worry me. I wasn't bothered much, me. It's funny, paedophiles, like, they're the same. Like, if they like, like you when you're fourteen, that's OK. But they're really on somebody who likes nine-year-olds. They're just like anyone else.

Andrew You have taken some action?

Terry No more than what you'd have to take against, my mother, my fucking father. That's alright though, innit. Keep it in the family.

Andrew What have you taken?

Terry No. I don't do drugs. Now. I never done much. Done bit a gear. But I never got . . . I got more sense.

I don't drink. A lot do E. The weekend. You know, that's all.

I'd like to kiss you. I would. Straight. I would. Do you want me to fuck you? Do you want to fuck me? I don't mind. I'm coming down. I'm feeling very, you know, like . . .

I'd like to see you. Can I see you?

Andrew You are seeing me.

Terry Come off it.

Andrew Yeah. You can see me. But you won't come round.

Terry If I don't come round, you'll know you can never trust me again. Come on.

NINE

David.

David I took my mother to the Tate for lunch and because she wanted to see the new hang. Hello Mother. How was your train? Where's Mrs Oakley? She usually has her friend with her. They come up to town together as a team. I don't think she likes what she sees. I can't tell. I think she thinks it's her duty. They usually make straight for the Royal Academy. Do you want to see the Pre-Raphaelites now, Mother? No, dear, not yet. And she stands assessing whatever is the most question-able new acquisition there. Installations are what take her particular attention. She usually sniffs at them and says, interesting. And I know she wants to see Ophelia Drowning – because she's sent me a postcard of it twice. Then we have lunch and then a matinee. I couldn't face it.

She usually has Mrs Oakley with her. They're old campaigners. They been at it for years. Forays every month or so. Matinees now because of the trains. Did you like the play, Mother? Very interesting, dear. Are you sure you don't need a taxi? No, dear, no. No need. How's Christopher, she says at some point. Goodbye dear. She says, even brighter then.

I don't think I'm incompetent enough. She prefers my brother, who's a hopeless drunk or you because you've done something interesting. I think I challenge her competence. It's as though she's jumped a generation. She's quite from another time. See you soon, dear. When will you be down? Daddy would love it. Daddy wouldn't love it. Daddy couldn't care less. I don't know why I'm being so ungenerous. She's a really good woman. It's just seeing her on the train always makes me think of going back to school.

TEN

Tony and Christopher.

Tony Nice motor.

Christopher Would you like to buy it?

Tony I would. But I wouldn't have the price. Do you want anything?

Christopher You've got a dog.

Tony Do you want a drink? A beer?

Christopher I'm driving.

Tony Well, you're not going yet, are you? You can have a beer. Are you?

Christopher I ought to go.

Tony Why did you give me a lift then?

Christopher Because you like the car. You wanted a lift.

Tony I wanted more than a lift, mate.

Christopher You've had more than a lift.

Tony Yeah. I know. But that was a bit, well.

Christopher Public.

Tony Yeah. And I couldn't see.

Christopher It's not that I don't want to, but . . .

Tony Why did you come in?

Christopher I know. I shouldn't have.

Tony What's the matter? You playing away from home? You married? Are you? Is that it?

Christopher Yeah. I am. Just at the moment and I shouldn't. Are you on your own?

Tony Yeah. Yeah. I am just at the moment. I'm just shagging and drinking at the moment. I'm going to get pissed tonight.

Christopher Why?

Tony Something to do.
    You been there before?

Christopher No I haven't. It's quaint, isn't it?

Tony Yeah. It's too handy for me. Near the station. Persuade myself I need a sauna after the long slog. You?

Christopher I was showing the car to someone and I couldn't sell it. There's a classic car garage in one of the arches.

Tony What is it?

Christopher A Hispano Suiza.

Tony Cracking motor.

Christopher I don't think I'll be able to get a price for it though.

Tony You want to stay down here?

Christopher No. Don't make me feel . . . I should go.

Tony No. You don't want to go. She won't know.

Christopher I know she won't.

Tony You coming up?

Christopher I'm so weak.

ELEVEN

Terry and Robert.

Terry I come round. I never phoned because I lost your number. I didn't know whether you'd be in. I was lucky. See, I'm always lucky. I'll bring you luck. Aint you pleased to see me?

Robert Should I be?

Terry I couldn't explain. I want to explain.

Robert Explain then.

Terry See I had to have the money for something.

Robert I thought you had to pay the cab.

Terry I had me mate outside. There was rowing.

Robert Why didn't you come back?

Terry I know. I know. Bad, bad man.

Robert So what you round here for now? You haven't come round to pay it back, have you?

Terry Ain't you glad to see me? I bet you are. Ain't you?

Robert No. I'm not. Why should I be glad to see you?

Terry You are. I'll get you the money, somehow. I'll pay you back. No, I will. I just thought I'd ring the bell. I had to be down here. This way. I thought . . . I'll go if you like. Is that it? OK then. Well you could, like, give us a cup of tea. I'm parched.

Robert I could.

Terry Go on then. Come on, don't be like that. I'm really sorry, I am.

Robert Do you want any money? No, no. You need money, don't you?

Terry I don't want money.

Robert You do. That's why you're here. It's alright. Tell me, is that it?

Terry No, that's not why I'm here. No, no. That's not why I'm here. On my life.

Robert Doesn't matter. Here take it, go on.

Gives him money.

Terry I ain't got no money. I'm skint.

Robert I know. Go on, take it. It's alright.

Terry Thanks.

Robert Don't say anything. Now I'm going to throw you out. OK. I got things to do.

Terry No. Let me stay.

Robert No.

Terry Come on.

Robert No, no. I've got to begin work soon.

Terry So I got to go?

Robert Yeah.

Terry Alright then. So long, mate. I'll see you.

Robert I don't know whether you will.

TWELVE

Stewart and Michael.

Stewart I've been for a drink.

Michael Good.

Stewart I've got to have a piss.

Michael Good.

Stewart I feel sick.

Michael Great.

Stewart Michael.

Michael What?

Stewart Michael.

   Michael goes to him.

Michael Sit down, come on.

Stewart No it's alright, I'm alright thanks.

Michael You alright?

Stewart Yeah, you're a pal. I'm going for a piss OK.
What's the matter?

Michael Now I feel sick.

He bends over, his hands on his knees.

Stewart No, don't feel sick.

Michael I think I'm going to be sick.

Stewart No you're not.

Michael How do you know I'm not going to be sick?

Stewart Are you gonna be sick? Michael.

He goes to comfort Michael and leans over his back, resting.

Don't be sick: I'm not going to be sick. I'm never sick. Are you alright Michael? Oh, Michael, I'm going for a piss. You coming for a piss? I feel rotten. I'm gonna put my fingers down my throat.

Michael Now I feel really sick.
Or . . .
What is it?

Stewart Leave it out will you.

Michael Hang on. Hang on. Hang on!

Stewart Just leave it.

Michael What's the matter?

Stewart You are.

Michael Or . . .

Stewart I'm going for a drink.

Michael Oh yes.

Stewart Yes.

Michael Oh Christ!

Stewart Yes.

Michael Look, why don't you go for a drink?

Stewart I am going for a drink.

Michael Well go for a fucking drink then.
Or . . .
Are we going to the pictures then?

Stewart I don't know.

Michael Well do you want to go to the pictures?

Stewart I don't know, why should I have to make all the fucking decisions?

Michael Well why should I have to?

Stewart Well why should I?

Michael Don't shout.

Stewart I'll shout.

He sits on the floor.

Michael What is it?

Stewart I'm fucking confused, I can tell you. I've never felt like this before, I can tell you. About any fucker.

Stewart is crying.

Michael Why?

He kneels by Stewart and puts his arms round him.

Why?

Stewart Get off.

Stewart pushes him away, Michael follows him. Stewart turns in to Michael briefly then pushes him violently away again.

73

You're so fucking clever you are, you ought to be done away with, you. You're sick. D'you know that? You're sick. You're sick, d'you know that. You're sick. You are. You're really sick. You're sick. You really are.

Michael Don't.

Stewart Do you love me? You love every fucker you do.

Michael Come on. Come on, let's go to the pictures.

He takes Stewart by the elbow.

Come on.
  Or . . .

Stewart I have to thank you. No. I do.

He grabs hold of Michael.

No, don't fuck about. Thanks. Thanks. Hold still. Thanks.

Michael Or . . .
  Hello. Nice to see you.

Stewart Don't start anything.
  Don't Michael. Alright?

Michael Very nice.

Stewart I've put the kettle on.

Michael I've been everywhere looking for you. I've been to the pub. I've been to the Irish pub. I've been to all the snooker halls round here. I've been to Sid's Snooker Saloon. You looking for Stewart, you've just missed him. I've been down Portobello to see if you were scoring. I've been in the Elgin, I've been down All Saints Road. I went over to Cold Harbour Lane. All up the Railton Road. I came back here again. I nearly rang the law. I've had a really good time. You?

Stewart What you go over there for? I haven't been over there. How long is it since I've been over there?

Michael I don't know. Where have you been?

Stewart Look I was on the piss. I didn't think I'd better come back.

Michael Where'd you end up?

Stewart I don't know.

Michael You know.

Stewart I don't. Look, it's none of your business where I've been, where I ended up.

Michael Just tell me.

Stewart I'm not telling you, Michael. And if you were so concerned you should have shown some concern earlier. I can go out by my own if I want to, OK? Anyway, I asked you to come with me. I wanted you to come. I'm not staying here with you pulling me to pieces one minute and not talking to me the next. You talk about commitment. You haven't spoken to me for three days. What am I to do?

Michael Why didn't you ring up?

Stewart Because I didn't want to.

Michael I'll pull it on, I will, one of these days.

Stewart Well, you wanted me to go out. Didn't you eh? Didn't you?

Michael I didn't.

Stewart Didn't you?

Michael I didn't.

Stewart Oh yeah. Well, why wouldn't you talk to me?

Michael Where were you, tell me. Please.

Stewart And anyway, what about you, eh? What about you?

Michael What?

Stewart You know.

Michael I don't know. What? There was an old man dying. I worked on.

Stewart You didn't tell me.

Michael Did you mind then?

Stewart No, of course I don't mind. But you didn't tell me.

Michael You haven't said anything about it since.

Stewart Well I'm saying it now. I had to ring and find out where you were.

Michael You didn't tell me.

Stewart To find out if you were working on. I had to make a right fool of myself.

Michael How was that making a fool of yourself?

Stewart Well it was.

Michael Well what do you think I was fucking doing last night? And I haven't been to sleep. And I've got to be up all tonight.

Stewart Now you know what it's like.

Michael Stewart, I worked all night because an old man was dying and they were shorthanded and I spent most of the day with him and I worked on.

Stewart You're stupid you are, anyway.

Michael What do you mean?

Stewart You're more qualified than what any of that poxy lot are. What's the matter with you! You've had an education. You give up a top job in the civil service and now you're a hospital fucking orderly.

Michael Auxiliary.

Stewart And how long's it gonna last?

Michael What?

Stewart What are you going to do next?

Michael What are you going on about? What am I going to do next? What about you? What are you doing? What do you do all day? Sleep, boozer, betting shop, smoke dope, sleep.

Stewart But Michael, you haven't got the necessary to be a tosser like me. What are you doing?

Michael Leave me alone.

Stewart But you're making a mess of yourself.

Michael I'm tired.

Stewart Why'd you give your first job up, eh?

Michael I don't know.

Stewart Why? Tell me.

Michael Don't. Please. Really.

Stewart Go on.

Michael I think I thought it was wrong. And you know . . . Growth.

Michael laughs.

I wanted to do something connected with people.
Where were you?

77

Stewart No.

Michael You've got to tell me.

Stewart I haven't.

Michael Tell me.

Stewart No.

Michael Alright. Put the kettle on.

Stewart It's on.

Michael Go on.

Stewart It's on, it's on. Do you want me to sing to you?

Laughter.

Michael Where were you?

Stewart You'll never find out.

Michael I will.

Stewart I doubt it. Got a paper?

Michael There.

He gives Stewart a newspaper.

Stewart Oh Christ, I've got to change. Have you got any clean underpants?

Michael I've stopped wearing them. They're bad for you.

Stewart Oh aye.

Michael Am I making the tea?

Stewart I don't know. Are you?

Michael Are you?

Stewart I will if you like.

He drops the newspaper.

Michael I'll do it.
   Where were you? Tell me.

Stewart Michael. No.

THIRTEEN

Terry and Andrew.

Terry Why won't you talk to me?

Andrew I don't know why I let you in.

Terry I know why you let me in.

Andrew No you don't.

Terry Don't I? No. I'll go then. I only thought we could have a drink, like. Have a few beers. You know. How's your mum?

Andrew Don't ask me about my mum.

Terry No, no. I won't. I lost your number. I did. I did.

Andrew I know you did.

Terry I did. Well, what's the matter then?

Andrew It's no good. It's no good.

Terry I don't know what I'm going to do. I been on the rob again. I ain't got no money. I ain't got no one. I ain't got nowhere.

Andrew Where you sleeping?

Terry Here and there.

Andrew This is no good. Honest. I'm sorry.

Terry I ain't got no one. I'd like to have you. I'd like to be with you. Don't get rid of me. You want me to go.

Don't you? Why? Look. I brought something. I'll protect you.

Andrew Don't.

Terry You liked it. You wanted me to fuck you. I liked it. You're exciting. You wouldn't keep still. Your pukka. I'm good at loving, I am.

Andrew No.

Terry I'll shoot off then. Is that it? Is that it, like?

Andrew Yeah.

Terry Well, yeah. I'll fuck off then. Fuck off then you. Alright. Fuck off. You don't know nothing, you don't. I'm fucking off. Fuck you.

Andrew No. Don't.

Terry Fuck off mate.

Andrew Don't.

Terry Am I staying, then?

Andrew No.

Terry Fuck off, then. I'll be alright.

FOURTEEN

David is sitting reading a letter. Christopher is standing.

David Does Jamie have to wear a kilt?

Christopher No. Why should he have to wear a kilt?

David I don't know. Or velvet.

Christopher No. What's the matter with you? It's only some ceremony in the garden. It's not a wedding. Don't you want to go?

David Not much.

Christopher Well you said you did. You said we had to.

David That's because you said you wouldn't go.

Christopher Oh and because I didn't want to go, you thought I should.

David Well you should go. Jamie wants you to go.

Christopher He wants you to go.

David It's a very nice letter.

Christopher Is it?

David It is. It is, Christopher.

Christopher If you say so.

David It just is.

Christopher Have you seen the invitation?

David No, where is it? Where is it?

Christopher Don't bully me.

David I'm not.

Christopher Just don't.

David You've got to stop this.

He finds the invitation.

I'd have thought they'd have used recycled paper. What is it?

Christopher Don't . . .

David Oh come on.

Christopher Don't.

David Right.

Christopher Sorry.

David Do you want a drink?

Christopher Do you want me to get it?

David She's had the baby.

Christopher Who?

David Mrs Murray. Who else do you know who's having a baby?

Christopher When? You didn't say.

David You didn't ask.

Christopher Oh thanks.

David The husband's a nice chap. At the delivery he fainted. We said it might be difficult. The baby was in distress. Thank God the midwife wasn't the senior midwife. She makes me feel hopeless. We couldn't get hold of the boss or the senior registrar. So I had to deal with it. It was a girl. Safe as houses.

Christopher picks up the invitation.

Christopher What about this? What are you wearing to this? What are you going to wear?

David Shorts.

Christopher No, you can't wear shorts.

David I don't know.

Christopher Wear your linen suit.

David What are you wearing?

Christopher Jeans.

David You can't wear jeans.

Christopher I can wear jeans. It's only in the garden.

You're the most exciting person I've ever met. And the most exhausting. When you're interested, you really are interested. You never forget anything I've ever said about myself – you make me feel I belong to you in some way. As though I'm part of you and I don't like it. Because. Well, it's as though I'm some extension of. That I'm some territory you know very well and are angry at losing. Some part of an empire. And your jealousy is frightening because it makes me feel I don't exist and responsible and angry. That it has nothing to do with me. And I could do without it. I really could. I don't want to feel so important. But you make me feel important in a way I've never felt. As though everything I've thought was something I had to be accountable for. But I sense your loyalty. Somehow I feel it's like a creed – political, religious. I can't imagine not knowing you now. You'd always be there fighting.

David We have to answer this.

Christopher Do we really have to go?

David Yes.

Christopher What's her name?

David Who?

Christopher Mrs Murray.

David Mrs Murray.

Christopher No her name.

David Don't know.

Christopher Do you want a drink?

David Yeah.

Christopher What's she going to call the baby?

David Mrs Murray? Well, she isn't going to call her after me.

FIFTEEN

Stewart and Michael.

Stewart I'm going.

Michael Why?

Stewart Ask yourself.

Michael Where will you go?

Stewart Don't worry about me.

Michael Or . . .

Stewart I don't know what I'm doing here.

Michael Don't you?

Stewart Cut it out, Michael, will you?

Michael Well what did you say that for?

Stewart Because I don't.

Michael Why don't you?

Stewart I don't know.

Michael Why?

Stewart Stop it, Michael, will you?

Michael I don't think this is perhaps what we had in mind.

Stewart I didn't have anything in mind. I think it was you who had things in mind.

Michael Or . . .

Stewart I'm going.

Michael Don't do that.

Stewart No I'm going.

Michael Where will you go?

Stewart Don't worry about me.

Michael I won't.
  Or . . .

Stewart This is stupid this is.

Michael What is?

Stewart This is.

Michael Not as stupid as you. I can't do this. This is hopeless. You're so stupid.

Stewart Hey you.

Michael What? What? I'm not scared of you.

Stewart Not yet you're not.

Michael What?

Stewart Alright. Alright.

Michael Or . . .
  I thought you were going.

Stewart I am going.

Michael I'm glad to hear it.

Stewart I am.

Michael Well go then, fuck off then.

Stewart I will.

Michael Well go on! Go on! Why don't you just go!
  Or . . .

Stewart What is it? Oh blimey, Charlie, shall I come
over there?

Michael Oh Christ no!

Stewart I want to.

Michael Well I don't. This is like . . . I don't know what
this is like. Like . . . this is.

Stewart Don't Michael.

Michael I'm alright. Don't come over.
  Or . . .

Stewart I'm moving out.

Michael Don't do that.

Stewart No, I'm going.

Michael Where will you go?

Stewart Don't worry about me.

Michael Why do you want to do that?

Stewart Why do you think?

Michael Or . . .

Stewart See, I can't handle it. I don't know what I'm up
to.

Michael I see.

Stewart Can't you see what I mean?

Michael No.

Stewart Well, I'm not up to it. That's for sure.

Michael Or . . .

I suppose one person can't be held responsible for the effect he has on another, wouldn't you say?

Stewart No, I wouldn't say. I bloody wouldn't say.

Michael Or . . .

Stewart I'll be off then. OK. Is it OK?

Michael What are you asking me for?

Stewart Well come with me.

Michael Or . . .

Stewart Be nice Michael. Be nice.

Michael Or . . .

Stewart Why do you want me to go?

Michael I don't.

Stewart But you do, Michael. I'll go if you'll say.

Michael I don't.

Stewart You do.

Michael I don't! I don't! I don't!

Stewart You see.

Michael Or . . .
Please.

Stewart No, for Christ's sake.

Michael I'll try.

Stewart No.

Michael I will.

Stewart You try.

Michael It's worse for me.

Stewart Oh yeah.

Michael I didn't mean it like that.

Stewart Oh.

Michael Don't go.

Stewart I've got to.

Michael It is possible.

Stewart I know.

Michael It basically seems to depend on whether you can do the washing-up. I'll do the washing-up.

Stewart Oh blimey. I haven't got it, Michael.

Michael Or . . .

Stewart Let's sort it out, shall we?

Michael Or . . .
  Or . . .

Stewart What do you want to do then?

Michael Or . . .

Stewart Am I staying?

Michael Or . . .

Stewart Come on, let's go.

Michael Or . . .

Stewart We'll be alright.

Michael Or . . .

Stewart What do you want?

Michael Or . . .

Stewart Just tell me!

SIXTEEN

Tony and Andrew.

Andrew How's the dog?

Tony He's alright. He's fine. My mother's looking after him.

Andrew But he's your dog.

Tony I know. She's got him for a few days.

Andrew See. See.

Tony What?

Andrew I knew you wouldn't feed him.

Tony He's been fed. My mother's fed him. You coming back?

Andrew What are you asking me?

Tony Don't. How can you stay here? Look at it.

Andrew Yes.

Tony I'm sorry.

Andrew I know.

Tony But I am. I'm sorry. I shouldn't have done it.

Andrew Don't keep on. I'm not asking you to say you're sorry. I don't want to hear about it again and again.

Tony Well, that's what started all this.

Andrew Is it?

Tony Isn't it?

Andrew I don't honestly know.

Tony Am I to say sorry for the rest of my life?

Andrew Look, no. Leave me alone.

Tony Well, what's going to happen? Is that going to be it? Don't you miss me . . . at all?

Andrew Yes. Don't be stupid.

Tony Come home. Come back with me. Now.

Andrew No.

Tony You can't stay here for good. You don't like it here.

Andrew We're going to have to sell it.

Tony Well, what you going to do?

Andrew I feel it will always get out of hand.

Tony And you don't want to risk anything.

Andrew I'm angry about what I can't change and what it is you still find in me. I can't find anything any more. I haven't the strength to go unprotected any more.

Tony Don't say that. I've thought, get someone else.

Andrew Have you?

Tony But it's not like that, is it? It's not finished between us. I feel this grief. I should let you go. I'm holding you back. Aren't I? Is that what it is?

Andrew Hold me back. What? I'm going nowhere. I'm so tired of making sense of the senseless. I don't know what I'm trying to do. Accept you for what you are. Which means what? I can accept you for what you are. You can't accept me you can't. I can't accept me.

Tony I don't know what I'm ever going to do without you.

Andrew You will.

Tony I won't.

Andrew You don't have to do without me. I'm not going anywhere.

Tony I was in bed last night and I started involuntarily to think about you.

Andrew Oh, just last night.

Tony It's every morning. I wanted to talk to you.

Andrew What about?

Tony I simply had things to say. Now I've fucked everything up.

Andrew What did you have to say?

Tony Don't be like this. It's not like you. You're not like this. Show some feeling. Come on. Let me. Let's find a way. Teach me. Show me. Please, Andrew. I'm lonely. I'm lonely without you.

Andrew Don't.
  I'm not coming back.

Tony Don't be like this. What is it?
  I can change.

Andrew I don't want you to change.

Tony What do you mean, you don't want me to change, what's all this?

Andrew Not change. You can't ask someone to change. I didn't ask you to change. You're alright.

Tony How can I be alright? Look what's happened.

Andrew Perhaps I could change. But I don't think you can change back. You're alright as you are.

Tony But how can I be alright as I am? Because I want me to change. I want to change because if I don't I won't have you. But what am I to change? But I don't know how to change.

Andrew I never wanted you to change.

Tony You did.

Andrew I never said change. Did I ever say change? Don't change.

Tony Don't cry. Come back with me. It's alright. I know. I know. But can I see you? Is that it?

Andrew Yeah. Yeah.

Tony I want to fuck you.

Andrew Oh yeah?

Tony Don't. I do.

Andrew Yeah.

Tony Don't.

Andrew Yeah.

Tony Can I?

Andrew Yeah.

Tony Now?

Andrew Yeah.

Tony What, here?

Andrew Yeah.
But I'm not going back.

SEVENTEEN

Stewart and Michael.

Stewart Why didn't you ring?

Michael Couldn't.

Stewart Who brought the letter?

Michael Me.

Stewart You.

Michael I didn't think you'd come.

Stewart Why didn't you think I'd come?

Michael You're pretty diffident. Hence the note.

Stewart You should have rung me. Idiot.

He laughs.

Fool.

Michael You don't ring me. But I'm grateful all the same. Thanks. Honest. Thanks for coming, thanks. Thanks.

Stewart How have you been?

Michael Fairly fucking dreadful.

Stewart Not so bad then.

Michael You?

Stewart Oh me. Of course. You know me.

Michael Don't you want to know?

Stewart What?

Michael Why the letter?

Stewart If you like.

Michael Listen, this is important.

Stewart I know, Michael. Honest, why do you think I've come over, eh? Oh Jesus, listen. There's more at stake for me, you know.

Michael Oh aye.

Stewart Because you'll eventually get fed up with all this. Bound to. And where will that leave me, eh? Can you answer me that? You alright?

Michael I'm alright. You alright?

Laughter.

Stewart I brought this back.

He gives Michael a book.

Michael Did you like it?

Stewart Quite.

Michael I can't see why you couldn't have come round. What a bastard thing to do. Why don't you come round? I just can't bear the feeling that you're not coming round. That I'm not going to see you. But what would happen if you did come round? And yet there have been times in the last week when I have so wanted you to be here. Sitting here. When I've thought of things to say to you. Nothing much. Why? Why? But I'm no better than you, that's the truth of it.

You'd better go, hadn't you?

Stewart I suppose.

Michael Hadn't you?

Stewart If you want me to.

Michael Will you be alright?

Stewart I'll be fine. I'll ring you.

Michael Will you?

Stewart I will. Honest.

Michael But will you?

Stewart I said I would.

Michael You got the number. Where's the number? You got the number.

Stewart I've got the number.

Michael Where's the number? Oh Jesus.

Stewart Shall I ring you?

Michael If you want.

Stewart Do you want me to?

Michael If you like.

Stewart You've still got all these books then?

Michael Do you want to come in?

Stewart Shall we go then?

Michael What's your name?

Stewart Do you want a drink?

Michael Not very far.

Stewart By yourself.

Michael Not very often.

Stewart Where do you live?

Michael No. I don't.

Stewart Where's your jacket?

Michael I don't want to hurt you.

Stewart Are you a student?

Michael Or . . .

Stewart Michael.

Stewart doubles up in pain. Michael holds him.

Michael, it's hurting, it's hurting.

Michael It's alright.

Stewart Michael.

Michael It's alright.

Stewart Michael.

Michael It's alright.
Or . . .

Stewart Come on.

Stewart pulls Michael by the arm.

Michael No.

Stewart Yes. Come on. Come on. Come on!

Michael No.

Stewart Come on.

*There is a violent struggle between Michael and
Stewart, during which Terry stands and calls looking
as at a window.*

Terry Are you in? Let me in. Let me in. Are you in? Let
me in. Let me in. Let me in.

Michael and Stewart have stopped struggling.

Stewart It's alright.
Do you want to leave it then?